The Avro Arrow Story

The Impossible Dream

D0910827

by Bill Zuk

To all the Avroites, especially my dear friend, Janusz
Zurakowski who left us in 2004 for a final flight.

PUBLISHED BY ALTITUDE PUBLISHING CANADA LTD.
1500 Railway Avenue, Canmore, Alberta T1W 1P6
www.altitudepublishing.com
www.amazingstories.ca
1-800-957-6888

Based on a book with the same title
by Bill Zuk first published in 2004

Extreme care has been taken to ensure that all information presented in
this book is accurate and up to date. Neither the author nor the
publisher can be held responsible for any errors.

Publisher	Stephen Hutchings
Associate Publisher	Kara Turner
Junior Edition Series Editor	Linda Aspen-Baxter
Edited by	Linda Aspen-Baxter & Frances Purslow
Cover and Layout	Bryan Pezzi

We acknowledge the financial support of the Government
of Canada through the Book Publishing Industry Development
Program (BPIDP) for our publishing activities.

Altitude GreenTree Program
Altitude Publishing will plant twice as many trees as were used
in the manufacturing of this product.

ISBN 10: 1-55439-703-0
ISBN 13: 978-1-55439-703-7

Amazing Stories® is a registered trademark of Altitude Publishing Canada Ltd.

Printed and bound in Canada by Friesens
2 4 6 8 9 7 5 3 1

Note: Words in **bold** are defined in the glossary at the back of the book

Contents

.

Prologue

The date was April 18, 1958. The CF-105 Arrow streaked toward Lake Superior. A burst fired from its afterburners. It increased speed past the sound barrier. Then it zoomed straight up. Janusz "Zura" Zurakowski was the Avro test pilot. He planned to fly the aircraft faster and higher than ever before.

The CF-105 climbed higher. Zura carefully set the dual throttles at just below maximum power ...

High above, Zura stood the Arrow on its tail. He passed 50,000 feet. As he did, he pulled away from his chase planes. He was still increasing his speed. He eased back on the throttles. The CF-105 continued to climb. The Machmeter had reached 1.52 as the plane levelled out. The test flight was going well. Zura held station until the two chase planes came alongside.

Zura looked over at the other test pilots. Peter Cope was in the CF-100. Flight Lieutenant Jack Woodman was in the Sabr. Zura gave them both a big grin. They were flying in the Royal Canadian Air Force's (RCAF) latest fighters. The CF-105 had left them far behind during this test fight. What promise the Avro Arrow had!

Chapter 1
The Beginning of the End

L orne Ursel was one of Avro Canada's test pilots. He was flying a CF-100 Canuck model. As he flew over the Avro Aircraft plant at Malton, Ontario, he looked down. The parking lots were full. A huge crowd gathered at Hangar 1. No one wanted to miss this occasion. Sitting in Hangar Bay 1 was the Avro Arrow. It was October 4, 1957.

Ursel tested CF-100 fighters at the factory. They were tested before they were delivered to squadrons. Most experimental flying on CF-100s was routine. Sometimes, there were interesting aircraft to fly.

On this day, Ursel had drawn the CF-100 "trial

horse." It was being used to test the afterburning Orenda engine. This engine was meant for the Mk.6 version. The Mk.6 promised greater performance. The "reheat" or afterburner was new. It gave greater thrust than the standard Orenda jet engine.

The trial horse was a **hybrid** test "mule." It blended parts from different CF-100 Mk.4 and Mk.5 aircraft. It had been named "4 and one-half." It was easy to spot. It had extended tailpipes at the rear of the engines. The thrust in afterburning mode produced a loud roar to announce its arrival. The Mk.6 trial horse was not a favourite of the test pilots. The afterburners often did not light in a balanced way. This made it hard to control the plane.

Ursel saw more Avro Development test pilots overhead. Wladyslaw "Spud" Potocki and Peter Cope were in the sky. So was Chief Production Test Pilot Chris Pike. They were at the controls of CF-100 Canucks Mk.3, 4, and 5. The four fighter aircraft would show the Avro products to the large crowd below. While the Avro Arrow was rolled out, the test pilots would perform four high-speed flypasts.

The RCAF band was near the speakers' platform. At **1400 hours**, the band began to play, while onlookers filled the seats in front of Hangar Bay 1. Many important people attended. Officials from the parent company, A.V. Roe Canada, were there. **VIPs** came from the Canadian military, government, and aviation industry. Members of the U.S. Air Force (USAF) were also present.

The Avro Arrow rollout brought over 13,000 guests to the factory.

Frederick T. Smye was vice president of Avro Aircraft Limited. He spoke of how important the ceremony was to everyone at Avro. It was also important to Canada's aviation industry. The Arrow showed what Canadian technology could do.

Hugh L. Campbell was next to speak. He was air marshal and chief of air staff. He spoke about the Arrow's role in North America's air defence system. The aircraft would be able to meet and deal with any bomber threat to North America over the next decade.

Defence Minister George Pearkes reached up. He tugged on a golden **lanyard**. It was the signal to open the hangar doors. A small tow truck pulled the Arrow into the daylight. The crowd cheered and clapped. Photographers and reporters hurried forward. Everyone pressed closer to the aircraft. Jan Jurakowski circled the Arrow slowly. He was Avro's chief development test pilot and would be the first to fly the Arrow.

Company president Crawford Gordon Jr. talked to the media gathered there. He said the Avro Arrow was ready to be tested. This was not true. The Arrow was not ready for its flight test. The aircraft had no radar, no weapons, and no **avionics**. Many instruments still had to be packed into the Arrow's weapons bay. Engineers needed to set up a schedule for testing all systems on the ground. This testing would extend far into the next year. The rollout was simply to raise public interest and support.

As the rollout ceremony ended, a silvery globe moved high in the heavens. It blinked a steady signal to its launch headquarters in Soviet Central Asia. **Sputnik** had just finished its first orbit of Earth.

In Malton, an Avro engineer was listening to his car radio. Robert Lindley heard the first news of the Sputnik satellite. The radio broadcast outlined the historic flight of the Sputnik.

Lindley thought to himself, "That's it. They've destroyed our rollout!"

The next morning, the Sputnik story figured in newspaper headlines all over the world. Even in Toronto, the Sputnik grabbed more paper space than the rollout of the Arrow. That date was a turning point. The true impact of the Sputnik was still to come.

Chapter 2
In the Footsteps of Titans

Avro Canada came into being because of World War II. Canada began to get ready for war in 1939. Mackenzie King was the prime minister and C. D. Howe was in charge of the ministry of transportation. Howe was also the minister of **munitions** and supply. His department would deliver the weapons of war. It would provide the raw materials and set up manufacturing plants to build the weapons. It would create supply lines to get the weapons to the **Allies**.

During wartime, industry grew across the nation. More than 400 ships were built on both coasts. They ranged from ships for **convoy** duty to merchant ships.

Automobile and locomotive factories were changed over to arms and munitions factories.

National Steel Car Corporation was based in Hamilton. It produced railway cars. However, it began to make munitions in the late 1930s. National Steel set up a huge manufacturing facility in Malton. It would build the Westland Lysander Army aircraft. Later, it would make the Avro Anson light bomber/trainer. The RCAF would use it. So would Great Britain's Royal Air Force (RAF). The Malton plant became an aircraft factory. In fact, it became the largest pre-war aircraft factory in Canada.

In 1941, Great Britain's A.V. Roe (Avro) and Company Ltd. turned to Canada to build Lancaster bombers. The British Supply Council wanted to make sure there was a constant supply of this heavy bomber. To do that, it turned to North America. U.S. factories could not accept new orders, but Canada was interested.

The British Supply Council had an office in Washington, D.C. Howe and several others went to a meeting there on behalf of Canadian industry and the military. Howe's right-hand man, E. P. Taylor, was chairman of the meeting. He said that on a recent visit to England, he had spoken with Lord Beaverbrook. Lord Beaverbrook was the minister of aircraft production. He had pleaded with Taylor. He wanted Canada to produce the RAF's newest heavy bomber, the Lancaster. Howe and Taylor made arrangements. Production would begin in Canada.

National Steel Car in Malton had been tooling up to produce the American B-26 Marauder bomber. Instead, it got the Lancaster contract. Making the Avro "Lanc" would be a huge challenge. The rewards would be great for Canada. The Lancaster was the most respected British bomber of World War II. RAF, RCAF, and Commonwealth crews had flown it. It was used mainly in night raids. It had four Rolls-Royce Merlin engines and a sturdy **airframe**. The Lancaster could carry different loads of bombs. It carried the 22,000-pound "Grand Slam," which was the heaviest bomb carried by any aircraft during the war.

In 1943, there was a famous raid called the "Dam Busters" raid. Lancasters were **modified** for that raid. They flew at only 60 feet above water and skipped bombs into the dams of the Ruhr Valley in Germany. The RAF kept up the night bombing. In time, this bombing led to the defeat of the Nazis. The Avro Lancaster became a legend. It could survive enormous damage and still return its crews safely home.

Roy "Dobbie" Dobson can be given credit for the Lancaster. He was managing director at A.V. Roe. The design team, led by Roy Chadwick, created the technical drawings. They were responsible for the Avro (type 679) Manchester. It was the design from which the Lancaster sprang. However, it was Dobson who fought to launch the new bomber.

The Manchester had flown in 1939. It was a twin-

The Avro Lancaster (with RCAF markings).

engine aircraft. However, there were problems with its Rolls-Royce Vulture I engines. The engines kept failing. That meant a loss of aircraft. It also meant a short life in service. In 1940, A.V. Roe had to scrap the Manchester.

When Chadwick was told that the Manchester bomber was cancelled, he and a small engineering team went to work. They redesigned the Manchester and created a four-engine bomber. They used the fuselage of the Manchester, adding a larger version of its wing. This design did not use Vulture engines. It used proven Rolls-Royce Merlin engines. They called it the Manchester III.

Members of the ministry of aircraft production arrived at A.V. Roe in July 1940. Dobson wanted a chance to build this new design. Lord Beaverbrook told Dobson that no Merlin engines were to be released for experimentation. Dobson then appealed to Lord Hives, the director of Rolls Royce. Lord Hives gave Dobson the same answer as Beaverbrook. Merlins were needed for the Spitfire and Hurricane fighters. These aircraft defended Britain.

Dobson finally convinced Hives to "loan" him just four Merlins. They were swiped right off two **prototype** Beaufighter fighters. Dobson gave Chadwick the go-ahead.

The prototype flew for the first time on January 9, 1941. It was called the Lancaster. Beaverbrook learned of the successful trials of a new Avro bomber with Merlin engines. He was dumbfounded. The Lancaster was accepted by the British ministry.

Production of the Avro Lancaster came to Canada. The fate of the project was in the hands of two people. One was Dobbie from England. The other was C. D. Howe from Canada.

In 1942, National Steel Car Corporation became Victory Aircraft Limited. Victory Aircraft hired more staff and put together a production team. The plant began turning out airframes. The Canadian-built Lancaster X used a mix of British and U.S. equipment. The Packard Company in the United States provided Packard-Merlin power plants. The first British "pattern aircraft" arrived. KB700 became the first production Lanc. It flew on

August 1, 1943. KB700 was later code named LQ-Q. It was named "Queenie."

Victory's workforce increased production. They made one Lancaster a day until the end of the war. Equipment was improved because high standards were kept in assembly. In some ways, the Lancaster X was better than the British-built Lancaster. Finished bombers were flown across the Atlantic to units in the war. Only one was lost.

Dobson began to receive glowing reports from the plant. He decided to visit Victory Aircraft himself. He flew across the Atlantic in September 1943. Any ocean crossing at that time was dangerous. However, Dobson was determined to see the Malton factory.

Dobson had planned to watch the rollout of the first Lancaster built in Canada. Victory Aircraft didn't wait for him. By the time he arrived, KB700 was already doing test flights. Dobson was amazed at what was going on at Victory. Most people in Malton village were Victory employees. About 8000 men and women worked on three eight-hour shifts. Workers were proud of their work. There was a spirit of friendship at the plant. Although pay was only $1 an hour, workers could afford a home and a car.

Dobson met with aviation officials. He also met with government officials. Then he interviewed C. D. Howe. Dobson had a new idea.

* * *

It was June 12, 1944. A Lancaster Mk. X from Canada was on its fourth mission over France. Nazis occupied France at that time. The Lancaster, KB726, was code-marked "VR-A." It had been assigned to 419 Squadron of the No. 6 RCAF Bomber Group. The crew was Canadian, except for the flight engineer. He was Flight Officer (F/O) Roy Vigars. F/O Arthur de Breyne commanded the crew. The night before, the bomber had blown up the bridge and crossroads at Constances.

On this night, everything went wrong. Searchlights over Cambrai lit up the Lancaster. Anti-aircraft guns shot at the bomber. Pilot de Breyne corkscrewed the Lancaster away. He dropped down to 2000 feet. The tail-gunner was F/O Pat Brophy. He spotted a Junkers Ju-88 night-fighter. It was closing in. He shouted out a warning over the intercom. The Ju-88 slipped under the twisting bomber and fired. It hit the Lancaster twice in the port wing. Both engines were knocked out. The fuel in the wing tanks caught fire. The mid-gunner was Warrant Officer (W/O) Andrew Mynarski. A third cannon shell struck the fuselage. It hit between Mynarski's station and the rear **turret**, starting a hydraulic oil fire.

The blaze engulfed the bomber. Crewmen at the forward stations abandoned the aircraft. De Bryne kept trying to wrestle with the controls. Mynarski saw the bailout command but turned back to check on Brophy.

He could just make out the tail-gunner. The turret's escape door was jammed, and Brophy was struggling with it. There were flames down the corridor. That didn't stop Mynarski. He tried to help his trapped tail-gunner. Moments later, the fire reached his clothing and parachute. Brophy tried to wave him away, but Mynarski kept hacking at the turret with a fire axe. He even tried to pry it free with his bare hands.

Finally, Mynarski had to quit. He was ablaze from foot to waist. He stood at the escape hatch and saluted his friend. Then he jumped out of the bomber to his death. The tail-gunner was the only person left on board. The Lancaster crashed into a field and careened into a tree. The turret section was ripped away from the rear fuselage. The impact snapped the turret doors open. Brophy was thrown free of the exploding wreckage. His survival was a miracle. Andrew Mynarski was awarded the Victoria Cross after his death. It was the last medal of its kind presented to an airman in World War II.

Mynarski's story was only one of many tales of the Avro Lancaster. Between 1940 and 1946, 7400 Lancasters were produced in Great Britain and Canada. More than 9500 employees were hired to produce the Lancaster at Victory Aircraft Limited. By war's end, Victory had built 3634 Avro aircraft. There were 3197 Ansons, 430 Lancasters, 6 Lincoln bombers, and a single York airliner.

Chapter 3
Building the Team

I n September 1945, the last of the Lancaster X bombers rolled out of the assembly bay at Victory Aircraft. Crews knew it was more than the end of the production run. Victory Aircraft was finished. Only 300 workers remained. There were no new contracts.

Dobson tried in vain to drum up new contracts. He tried to sell new Lincoln bomber and York transports to the Canadian military. Both were developments of the Lancaster. He also tried selling them to the airlines. Pattern aircraft were constructed at Victory Aircraft. Neither project got past that point.

At Malton, layoff notices were ready for all employees. In the backrooms, Dobson worked to save the company. He sought out C. D. Howe, who was now the minister of reconstruction. Canada had to recover from the war. During the war, the economy had focused on the war effort. Factories and manufacturing plants had been geared to producing supplies for the war. Canada's economy had to develop in different ways after the war.

Dobson offered to purchase Victory and its huge factory. Howe hammered out an agreement with Dobson. The deal created a new company with a Canadian command. It had to carry out research and development in aviation. To do this, Dobson also acquired Turbo Research Limited. This was where the "Chinook" was designed and tested. It was Canada's first jet engine. The Nobel Test Establishment at Parry Sound was also thrown into the deal. A.V. Roe Canada Limited was born on November 2, 1945. It became known as Avro Canada. It had only one employee — Frederick Timothy Smye. Smye proudly wore Avro Employee Badge No. 1 until the end of his career.

The aircraft factory hired 300 former Victory Aircraft employees. Smye became the general manager. Smye put together the best possible workforce. The first contracts had nothing to do with aviation. The plant began turning out plastic hairbrushes, truck fenders, and tractor parts. The first aircraft contracts involved repair and overhaul work on Hawker Sea Fury fighters and B-25 Mitchell bombers.

Then came the first major contracts. Victory had to convert the remaining Lancaster bombers. The RCAF needed planes for coastal patrol and air search-

and-rescue. They also needed planes for **photo-reconnaissance**. They decided to pull the Lancaster aircraft out of storage. The heavy bombers were taken to the factory to be converted. This was the chance A.V. Roe needed. They could expand their operation.

Dobson assembled a talented design team. The Canadians included Stan Cyma, Jack Millie, Mario Pesando, and Bryan Wood from Victory. James A. Chamberlin came from Noorduyn Aircraft. English engineers Edgar H. Atkin, Robert N. "Bob" Lindley, and James C. "Jim" Floyd from A.V. Roe Limited (Manchester) became a part of the design team. So did John C. M. Frost from De Havilland (U.K.) and Waclaw Czerwinski from Poland.

Avro Canada designed their first project with one customer in mind. It was Trans-Canada Airlines (TCA). (TCA later became Air Canada.) This was C. D. Howe's "baby." Jim Floyd had drawn up blueprints while still in England. They were for a "30-seater Transport Aircraft." Now he and his design moved to Canada. H. J. Symington was president of TCA. He signed a letter of intent with Avro Canada. This letter outlined what had to be done.

The original design used two Rolls-Royce engines. However, Rolls-Royce refused to provide the AJ65 engines. The airliner was quickly redesigned. This version was powered by four Rolls-Royce Derwent engines. This type of engine was tried and proven. It was named the C102 "Jetliner."

When the production drawing stage was reached, TCA showed signs of "cold feet." Symington decided to approach C. D. Howe. Symington wanted TCA to be released from their letter of intent. He said there were technical issues in the redesign. The main concern was about the costs for this new airliner. By 1947, both Howe and Dobson were at a crossroads with Avro Canada. They faced triumph or disaster.

More than 200 engineers and technical staff worked in the design office. Two other projects were also under-way. All of the research and development work was in danger. Howe had to come to the rescue. He provided $1.5 million for development. It was enough to keep Avro Canada in business.

On the drawing board was the XC-100 fighter. Chief Engineer Edgar Atkin and Project Engineer John C. M. Frost designed it. The RCAF had called for a Canadian-designed fighter. It would be used to protect Canada's Arctic frontier. The XC-100 was Avro Canada's submission. It had a new jet engine called the TR-5 Orenda 1. This jet engine was based on the earlier Chinook design. (The Orenda would power all of Avro's future aircraft. It would be sold to other manufacturers and be very successful. Today, Orenda jet engine technology is all that remains of Avro Canada.)

Dobson gave Jim Floyd and his team the go-ahead. They were to complete the first Jetliner. They went to work on the CF-EJD-X. It was the Avro C102 prototype.

While preparing for its flight test, Avro was in a race with De Havilland Aircraft. Who would get the first jet-powered airliner into the air? In England, De Havilland was putting the finishing touches to the DH. 106 Comet.

Spring and summer of 1949 saw the final stages of taxi testing for both airliners. The Avro Jetliner missed being the first into the air. Malton airport was having its runways resurfaced. That got in the way. The engine housing had to be repaired at the last minute. These repairs delayed the Jetliner's maiden flight. Test pilot James "Jimmy" Orrell flew the C102 on August 10, 1949. The Comet had already been flying for 13 days. It was the world's first jet airliner. Floyd and Dobson had come in second.

When the first test flights were done, the Jetliner captured headlines all over the world …

* * *

Jim Floyd stared out the Jetliner's window at Manhattan's skyline. Fred Smye was sitting across from him. Floyd motioned to Smye to look out his window. The Jetliner flight from Toronto to New York had taken less than an hour. Pilot Don Rogers would log the flying time as 59 minutes and 56 seconds. His average speed had been 400 miles per hour. It was April 18, 1950.

Rogers entered the landing circuit for Idlewild Airport. (Today, it is Kennedy International.) He slipped in behind a Convair 240, a piston-engined transport. The Convair was one of the newest in the sky. Compared to the Avro C102 Jetliner, however, it looked like an antique. The Jetliner could operate routinely at 30,000 feet. It cruised at twice the speed of the latest piston airliners. The sleek silver and yellow jet aircraft was just over the edge of the city. It turned downwind. As it did, the tower picked it up. Mike Cooper-Slipper was in the right-hand seat. He had just relayed the message to Rogers that they were cleared to land.

Onboard the Jetliner, Bill Baker was smiling as he took out a glowing peace pipe. He was the flight engineer. Toronto Mayor Hiram McCallum had sent the peace pipe along with a massive scroll. On the scroll were greetings from the Canadian International Trade Fair.

Rogers made one pass over LaGuardia Airfield. Then he swept in to make a graceful landing. Reporters and photographers scrambled for the best spots. They joined a large group of officials. The crew appeared at the cockpit door. They wore bright white coveralls. Rogers was carrying a Native headdress. He held the smoking peace pipe. He would present it to a representative of the mayor of New York. The crew came down the steps to the bursts of flashbulbs.

The Jetliner had set many records with this flight. It was the first international jet airliner flight. It was the first time airmail had been delivered by jet. The Toronto postmaster had placed aboard a small sack of mail.

The Jetliner was a surprise to the United States. No U.S. competitor even existed on drawing boards. Over 500 newspapers and magazines covered the story of the Jetliner's visit. So did local radio stations. The New York trip was an exciting visit for Avro Canada. However, it did not lead to any sales.

Back at Malton, the XC-100 was nearly ready for its first flight. It had been renamed the CF-100. John Frost was working behind the scenes. He was trying to correct a deadly flaw. Jim Chamberlin was chief aerodynamicist. He had acted without telling Frost. There had been a problem with weight distribution. To solve the problem, he had moved the two jet engines back through the centre section of the aircraft. Chamberlin had notched the wing **spars** to fit the engines. The notches weakened the spar. This created a "soft spot." It allowed the wings to flex dangerously.

Squadron Leader Bill Waterton would be the pilot for the test flights. The CF-100 prototype #18101 was not really ready for its flight tests. Waterton flew the first CF-100 Mark 1, coded FB-D, on January 19, 1950. The spar was still weakened. It was dangerous. His next test flights showed just how dangerous.

Waterton was over Toronto. He was doing a show at the Canadian National Exhibition when he heard a crack "like a thunderbolt." Luckily, he was able to land the aircraft. The spar had to be repaired. Further flights were put on hold. Waclaw Czerwinski was the leader of the stress office. He led an engineering "blitz." He designed a strengthened pin-joint to fix the problem.

In the same year, the Orenda jet engine was tested. A modified Lancaster was used for these tests. The Lancaster carried two Orenda turbojets in pods. The in-flight testing of the Orenda engine was a success. The Orenda later powered all CF-100s. It also powered the Canadair Sabre series of fighters.

Don Rogers and Mike Cooper-Slipper were Avro's pilots. Bill Baker was the flight engineer. They made up Avro's flying team. They began setting records with the Jetliner all over North America. The Jetliner seemed to be a success story.

Floyd remarked, "The flight program went unbelievably well. Airline flight times were halved by the Jetliner on inter-city flights all over the U.S. and Canada. Many U.S. airline executives were carried on these flights. All were enthusiastic about the aircraft."

All three Avro Canada projects were "off the ground." Then Cold War tensions exploded. War began in Korea. Canada had a commitment to the conflict. C. D. Howe gave instructions to Avro. They were to "ramp up" the production of the CF-100 fighter. Without notice, he ordered an end to the Jetliner. It was a bad time for this decision. Avro was in contract talks with National Airlines, Trans World Airlines, and the USAF. Howe was determined. The CF-100 fighter program had to come first. Floyd watched the second Jetliner prototype being broken up at the back of the factory. He had tears in his eyes.

* * *

C. D. Howe had been watching Avro Canada's progress with alarm. Then, the RCAF told him news he didn't want to hear. The CF-100's operational use was delayed due to design problems. Howe blew up at Dobson. "Fix the problems with the CF-100 ... and do it now!"

Sir Roy Dobson knew what he had to do. He knew just the man to do it. Crawford Gordon Jr. arrived at Avro Canada in 1951. He was like a whirlwind. By the end of the year, he had reorganized the company. He made sure the planes were there when the military needed them. He saw Jim Floyd and Fred Smye as major talents. He gave Floyd control of the CF-100 program and removed Atkin as chief designer. He moved Frost to the special projects group. He divided the operation into two divisions. Smye became general manager of the aircraft division. He put the gas turbine division under Tom McCrae. Avro moved into series production of the CF-100 fighter. At the same time, it began planning what would replace it.

Chapter 4
Test Flying at Avro Canada

These are the stories of Avro Canada's test pilots. Don Rogers was chief test pilot with National Steel. Then he continued with Victory Aircraft during World War II. He headed the flight operations department. He directed all of the flights of the C102 Jetliner, CF-100 Canuck, and CF-105 Arrow test programs. As the chief development pilot of the Avro Lancaster series, he racked up thousands of hours in testing and ferrying missions. He was known as a precise and smooth flier, as well as a skilled manager. Rogers was the command pilot of all the unusual Lancaster variations. One of these was the wild and woolly Orenda engine test-bed. Two jet engines on the ends of the wings replaced the usual Merlin piston engines. They were powerful enough to make this the fastest Lancaster ever.

Although Rogers would never admit to it, the Orenda test-bed was used to "spook" the Americans. They were on alert across the border at Niagara Falls. The Lancaster would fly over Lake Ontario well below radar. Then it would pop up on the USAF radar scopes. This caused panic on the U.S. side. Who was the intruder? Tired, old Air National Guard P-47 Thunderbolts would be **scrambled**. Then the Orenda Lancaster would fire up the jets and "squirt away" with no effort. The USAF was not amused by the Avro stunts.

The pilots flying this test-bed had another favourite trick. They shut down the Merlin engines and swept over an airfield powered by only the jet engines. The aircraft was nearly silent as it swooped and twirled away. Spectators on the ground were amazed.

Thomas Paul "Mike" Cooper-Slipper was Rogers' second-in-command. He flew with Rogers on all of the Jetliner demonstration flights in Canada and the United States. Rogers became the primary pilot in the CF-100 program.

Cooper-Slipper flew as a test pilot in England before he came to Canada in 1947. He joined Avro first as an engine fitter, then moved on to flight testing. He was the first post-war test pilot at Avro Canada. Cooper-Slipper

Avro CF-100 Canuck fighters on patrol.

began flying overhauled B-25 Mitchell and Lancaster aircraft. Then he was assigned to the Jetliner and CF-100 programs. Later, he became chief test pilot at Orenda Engines, Avro's sister operation. There, Cooper-Slipper did the development testing of the Orenda engine.

Mike was flying the Orenda Lancaster during an air demonstration over Malton. It wasn't planned, but he also became the pilot of the first Avro "glider." He buzzed the field in the usual way, flying only on jets. He shouted out to start the Merlins. Instead, his engineer shut down the jet engines. He had no altitude to spare. Luckily, Cooper-Slipper managed to relight the jets. Before that, the spectators got a close-up look at a completely silent Lancaster bomber gliding by!

Cooper-Slipper flew all of the CF-100 versions. He also flew the Orenda-powered Canadair Sabre. For a time, the RCAF Sabre squadrons flew the world's best fighter. Then, the CF-105 Arrow entered flight-test. Mike was assigned to the converted Boeing B-47 bomber. It was fitted with the mighty "Iroquois" test engines.

During the early period of test flying at Avro Canada, a pair of top guns joined Rogers and Cooper-Slipper. These two test pilots could not have been more different.

Jimmy Orrell was soft-spoken and thoughtful. He was on loan from Avro in England. There, he had tested the Avro Lancaster, York, and Tudor. He had been an RAF pilot and an Imperial Airways pilot. His work with them was mainly with large transports, but he also had experience with jet aircraft.

The Jetliner was finished on July 25, 1949. Orrell was ready to go down in the history of test flight. He missed his opportunity by days. An extended engine test was done. A problem with the jet exhausts was discovered. While the problem was being fixed, Avro's rival, the De Havilland Comet, had made a short test hop. De Havilland beat Avro to the punch.

Orrell carried out 16 test flights with the C102

Jetliner. The only mishap in testing occurred during the second flight. Orrell was setting up the prototype for a landing approach when the undercarriage refused to budge. Bill Baker was the flight engineer. He ratcheted the emergency gear-down handle in the cockpit. Nothing happened. Baker worked the gear-down handle so hard, he broke several ribs. He didn't even notice. The engineering staff on the ground worked frantically. They could not come up with any solutions. Jim Floyd was the chief engineer. He asked the pilot-in-command if he had any thoughts on the subject. Orrell didn't hesitate. He spoke drily over the intercom, "Our Father, which art in heaven ..."

The Avro officials on the ground tried to figure out what to do. They were worried about the fate of their crew. They also didn't want to lose their prototype. Orrell kept his cool. He set up four separate approaches. Each time he tested a combination of speeds, flap settings, and controls. Then he drifted in on a crosswind. He put the Jetliner down next to Malton Airport's east-west runway. He eased the aircraft onto the grass in a nose-up skid. It slid gracefully to a halt.

Floyd and the other engineers examined the aircraft. They were amazed. The underside had only slight damage. Jimmy had saved the company.

Then Orrell left Canada and another test pilot arrived at Malton. It was Squadron Leader William A. "Bill" Waterton. He had been a wartime RAF fighter pilot, instructor, and test pilot. He became a member of the RAF's World Air Speed Record team. He flew the Gloster Meteor at 616 miles per hour on September 7, 1946. Later in 1946, Waterton set the Paris–London speed record.

At Gloster Aircraft, Waterton worked on the Meteor, the RAF's first operational jet fighter. He was also a skilled aerobatic performer at the Farnborough Air Display. Waterton had tested the RAF's brand new design — the delta-wing Javelin. The Javelin nearly killed him. Part of the tail section broke off during a high-speed run. Only great skill and a stroke of luck saved his life. Skill and luck would come to his rescue once more at Avro Canada.

Waterton flew from Toronto to Boston in an Avro CF-100 prototype. He made the hop at an average cruise speed of 575 miles per hour. He and Bruce Warren landed at Logan Field on August 30, 1950. His aircraft was prepared for the upcoming air show. Its paint scheme was showy. It was gloss black with white lightning stripes. The Avro CF-100 was in a competition. The winner would become the next U.S. tactical fighter/bomber. The Boston Air Show would be a chance to show what it could do.

Waterton was disappointed. The air show committee would not allow **aerobatics** at the civil airport. All flying exhibitions had to take place over the Atlantic. Waterton knew that the crowd wouldn't get much of a show if he had to fly far out over water. He had spotted a tiny bay on the north side of the airfield. He spoke with the air show executive about using it. Waterton tried to convince them that he would be flying over water. They finally agreed that he could fly over the bay. He planned a tight routine.

Waterton's performance began. He blasted off in a full-throttle climb. The aircraft looked impressive in Waterton's hands. It climbed quickly. It also handled with ease. Waterton pushed the limits of the CF-100 further. The aircraft was just above the runway when he put the flaps down and the nose up. He hovered just above stall speed. Then he hit the throttles. The starboard engine stalled! He was at low altitude with almost no speed and flaps extended. He pushed down with all his might. He eased the fighter to a height where he could raise the flaps and carry out a single-engine landing. His actions saved his life. They also saved the aircraft.

Waterton worked hard in the CF-100 program. He took the prototypes from ground test to flight status. Some people thought he was too daring. Others thought he liked to exaggerate what the prototype could do.

Bill Waterton was eventually replaced by Flight Lieutenant Bruce "Duke" Warren. Warren was a noted RCAF test pilot. His time ended before it really began. Warren and his observer, Robert Ostrander, died in a crash on April 5, 1951. They were flying the second CF-100 prototype.

A small tube from Warren's helmet was later found in his desk at the plant. Like most pilots, he had cleaned his own oxygen mask that day. He had likely passed out when his oxygen mask failed. This matched reports from a Trans-Canada Airline crew. They had witnessed a black jet in a vertical dive straight into the ground. Warren and Ostrander were the first Avro Canada flight crew to give their lives. They were not the last.

In November 2000, a tobacco farmer found a small scrap of the cockpit frame. Mark Matthys lived near the crash site at Mount Brydges, Ontario. In the mud under the metal, he found a skull fragment. The impact of the aircraft had made a crater in the ground. For years, sheet metal shards had turned up in a field circling this crater. A smashed watch was found in a wooded area near the farm. On the watch was "Avro" and a serial number. Matthys contacted department of transport investigators. They searched the area. They turned up more remnants of the CF-100 accident. On April 5, 2001, the farmer placed a wooden cross and flag at the crash site. Matthys made a promise. On the anniversary date for the rest of his life, he would commemorate the passing of these gallant fliers.

Chapter 5
The Greatest
of Them All

It was Monday, September 5, 1955. The morning showers had lifted, and the sky brightened over Farnborough, England. Jan "Zura" Zurakowski was to fly the Avro CF-100 Mk.4b fighter at 1345 hours. Zurakowski would be doing a flight demonstration. It was the first day of the three-day Farnborough Air Show. There was a tight schedule at this world-class event. Each aircraft had to take off within 30 seconds of its chosen time. Zura did not want to miss his slot. He was strapped in and the twin Orenda engines were ticking over.

Without warning, the Avro CF-100 was asked to move into position. It was 12 minutes ahead of schedule. Zurakowski swung the fighter onto the taxiway. He punched both engines into full thrust. The CF-100 streaked down the main runway. Zura hit the undercarriage switch to raise the gear. As soon as the tires left the tarmac, it jumped into the air. He pointed the nose straight up. Then he wrenched the CF-100 into a vertical climb. He reduced power to idle on both power plants. The massive fighter sat transfixed in the sky for a moment. Then it slid downward gracefully tail first. Its slide lasted for a few hundred feet. Then Zura pushed over and pointed the nose to the ground. He swooped away, only a few feet above the runway. More than 100,000 spectators stared with wide eyes and open mouths.

One air show announcer exclaimed, "It's another Zurabatic!" Four years before, at the 1951 Farnborough Air Show, Jan Zurakowski had unveiled a new move. He had performed a cartwheel with a Gloster Meteor above the crowd. The aerobatic move had been called the "Zurabatic Cartwheel."

At the 1955 air show, Zurakowski showed off a number of tail-slides. Sometimes he added a "falling leaf" to the routine. In this move, the heavy fighter fluttered to the ground in a series of near-stalls. It looked like a leaf drifting down to the ground.

Zura added one more trick to his performance on the second flying day. He took off normally and then rolled the CF-100 on its back. When he hit the undercarriage button, the gear retracted downward. Zura twisted the aircraft back to normal and roared away.

Geoffrey Norris was from the RAF Flying Review. He described Zura's performance as "impossible, of course, but not for the Great Zura."

Fred Smye was vice president of Avro Aircraft Limited at that time. He was also general manager. He wrote Zurakowski to thank him. Smye called his display a "magnificent performance … the highlight of the show and a demonstration of flying skill which will long be remembered by those who were fortunate enough to be present."

Jan Zurakowski was making a name for himself as a skilled test pilot. He was also known as a superb aerobatic flier. Zura was Avro's most famous test pilot. His daring aerial routines put Avro in the world's headlines again.

Zurakowski had set world speed records when he worked for the Gloster Aircraft Company. He flew the Meteor, the RAF's first jet. He performed the first high-speed aerobatic photography flights. Crowds were dazzled by his aerial demonstrations at Farnborough. Few pilots have invented an aerobatic manoeuvre, but Zura did. The unique jet engine placement of the Gloster Meteor allowed him to do a "cartwheel." He throttled one engine back. Then he poured power into the other engine. That action made the plane seem to spin in place. The crowd in the 1951 Farnborough Air Show loved it.

Zurakowski tested the new Gloster Javelin in 1952. Then he wrote to Peter R. Cope to ask about the Avro

Canada operation. Cope was the new test pilot for the CF-100. Cope advised him to come to Canada.

Zurakowski resigned at Gloster and moved his young family to Canada. He became a test pilot for the CF-100. Jim Floyd was head of engineering. He was a fan of Zurakowski. Floyd called Zurakowski "a superb test pilot and the best acrobatic pilot in the world." He said that Zurakowski coaxed an aircraft to the limit of its performance. "He often took his mount [plane] beyond the accepted limits."

Many people had a story to tell about Zurakowski. His boss, Don Rogers, recalled that Zura knew the weight of an aircraft by instinct. One test involved loading up a CF-100. Zurakowski would take one look at the set-up and then announce the weight. When the technicians weighed the aircraft, they would shake their heads in wonder. Zura was always bang on.

Zura set up his own test routines to see what the CF-100 could do. Roy Combley flew with Zura on countless tests. He was Zura's flight observer. Combley was in awe. He declared, "I have never flown with a smoother pilot."

The **aileron** controls failed during one flight. Zura brought their CF-100 prototype in with them completely locked. Combley was amazed. He believed that no other pilot could have done that.

Zurakowski also knew a lot about mechanics. Bob Johnson was shop foreman. He tells of how Zura "pancaked" in with a collapsed landing gear. He insisted that the aircraft had retracted the main gear on its own. Mechanics couldn't find the fault. Zurakowski gave the fuselage a hard slap. Lo and behold, the CF-100 on the test stand raised its gear!

Chris Pike was a fellow test pilot. He told his friends how Zurakowski did the usual "walk-around" before a flight. Zura could just touch a part of the plane and announce that a part was missing. He would be right.

Another time, Peter Cope and other pilots were puzzled. They couldn't figure out why one of the test aircraft always dipped a wing in flight. Zurakowski stared at the wing. Then he took out a ruler. The ruler showed a gap between the leading edge and the rest of the wing. When that crooked leading edge of the wing was filled in, the aircraft flew perfectly!

When Zurakowski flew the Meteor for Gloster, he used to do formation aerobatic flying. A photographer in the cockpit had taken amazing aerial photographs of the Meteor. That had placed the Gloster products onto newspaper headlines around the world.

The aerial photographer at Avro Canada was Hugh Mackechnie. Zurakowski saw that Mackechnie liked to try new things. He also had a spirit of adventure.

Zurakowski talked Mackechnie into the back cockpit of a CF-100. Zurakowski showed him an array of aerial tricks. He trained a number of other test pilots to fly precision formation. Then he led them into aerobatic routines. Zurakowski always flew the camera ship. He would place the photographer in the best location for a great shot. He never failed. These aerial photos were great publicity.

Chapter 6
Pushing the Envelope

J an Zurakowski arrived at Avro Aircraft in 1952. His first task was to test fly the latest Avro CF-100. This aircraft was rated to go as fast as .85 Mach. It was generally believed that if a pilot flew the aircraft faster than its posted limit, he would not be able to control the fighter. Zura believed he could do it. He needed to find out if the CF-100 was safe at high-speed.

Zura began exploring the upper ranges of the flight speed. Diving from 40,000 feet, the CF-100 increased speed until the plane began to rock slightly. The air pressure was building up at the speed of sound. Zura looked down in amazement. He watched his Machmeter needle creep up to Mach 1. As it moved past Mach 1, there was a deafening boom. Zura was flying faster than the speed of sound. He had achieved supersonic flight. Very few pilots around the world had achieved this.

Zurakowski had to prove that the CF-100 was safe and reliable, even at supersonic speeds. Safety was vital. Sometimes Zura had to use unusual methods to make a point about safety. The company claimed that the CF-100's new heating and air conditioning system was okay, but Zura didn't think so. To prove his point, Zura took up an engineer when he tested the system. Zura didn't tell him what he was up to. Zura had put on extra sweaters and two pairs of thermal underwear. Then he cruised at high altitude for an hour. When he glanced back, the engineer was nearly frozen stiff. He had to be lifted out of the cockpit like a slab of frozen meat. The company quickly changed the heater after that.

In 1953, Brigadier General Bernard Montgomery, a British war hero, visited the plant in Malton. He asked to see what the latest CF-100 could do. Officials gathered near the airfield. Then Zura swept around a nearby hangar in a knife-edge pass just a few feet over their heads. The group scattered. Only Montgomery bravely faced the jet fighter as it rushed toward him. The general was impressed.

The day-to-day testing of the CF-100 continued. Each new version had to be tested. Soon, more staff were needed. Once again, Avro Canada turned to

England. Wladyslaw Jan "Spud" Potocki was testing the Avro Vulcan bomber at Avro (U.K.). He and Zurakowski had both served in 306 Squadron during the war years. Zurakowski had been the commanding officer. Potocki had been a sergeant-pilot. Like Zura, Potocki's flying career had begun with RAF wartime service. Then he had gone to the Empire Test Pilots' School. He was recruited to come to Canada.

More RCAF test pilots were assigned to the factory. Squadron Leader Ken Owen commanded a detachment that included Flight Lieutenants Jack Woodman, Reg Kersey, and N. "Norm" Ronaasen. Woodman had been the chief test pilot for the RCAF before he joined Avro as a test pilot. No one could match him as a pilot. A superb pilot, later he became the first Canadian selected for astronaut training.

Woodman was interviewed in 1978. "Flying with Don Rogers and the Avro team was an honour for me," he recalled. "I thoroughly enjoyed the four years I spent at Avro. I mentioned Zurakowski being the best test pilot I have ever known. The rest of the team, and all the Avro troops, were of the same calibre."

Zurakowski was thorough. He didn't miss a thing. His ground crew knew this. If an aircraft had a "snag," it was noted on the flight report. Zurakowski's reports were always detailed. If he wrote "NNS" on the margin, there were "no new snags." Zurakowski would find every "gremlin" that lurked in an aircraft. He would make sure that the aircraft would be safe to fly.

Safety for aircrews was his main concern. Testing could make the difference between life and death. If a CF-100 was damaged, the pilot and back seater had to eject. Ejecting had to be safe and reliable for both of them. Zura believed that the **canopy** would not detach properly. He flew countless tests. On each one, he blew canopies off their mounts. He kept testing them until he was satisfied.

Ejection tests with dummies had not proved that ejection procedures were sound. Zurakowski wanted live demonstrations. A Martin-Baker representative flew with him and ejected out of the back seat. Zura was still not certain.

Zurakowski was right to be concerned about ejection from a CF-100. It was August 23, 1954. A centrally mounted rocket pack was being tested. Zurakowski and his flight engineer came face-to-face with a deadly situation. They were high over the test range at Ajax, Ontario, when there was an explosion. Their test aircraft was crippled. Zurakowski began emergency procedures. He ordered his observer to eject.

A second explosion tore through the plane. Zurakowski ejected. He felt a searing pain in his right leg. The parachute opened above him, but his ankle was broken. He landed painfully in a farmer's field. It was seconds before the CF-100 slammed into the ground. Zura looked around. He couldn't see a second parachute. His observer hadn't made it. Hiebert had been trapped in the rear cockpit.

More tests were done. What had gone wrong? The first step in the ejection process was to pull down the face blind, but it had snagged. Testing showed that the blind would not release if it was tugged slightly off centre. This fault may have doomed Hiebert.

This tragedy would not happen again. Ejection procedures were changed. Ejection handles were added. They were mounted low on the seat. A lock-pin on Zurakowski's seat had been cut off. His seat had twisted sideways. His right leg slammed on the canopy rail as he left the aircraft. When Zura's broken ankle healed, he returned to flying.

The difficulty in ejecting out of a CF-100 would claim another life. Glen Lynes was a skilled test pilot. He had graduated from the Empire Test Pilots' School and had flown with the RAF and RCAF. He showed North Atlantic Treaty Organization (NATO) squadrons that were about to receive the CF-100 what the aircraft could do.

Lynes was on a routine test flight in one of the CF-100s. He got into trouble when he entered an inverted spin. He "punched out," but everything went wrong. Lynes never pulled the rip-chord on his parachute. He crashed to earth in front of Stan Haswell and Chris Pike. They were Avro test pilots who were waiting in line to take off. What had gone wrong? Lynes had ejected straight through the canopy, which broke his neck. In future, CF-100 pilots and aircrew would eject through the Plexiglas. A spike was mounted on top of the ejection seats.

In 1955, Jan Zurakowski became the chief development test pilot at Avro Aircraft Limited. He took over all experimental programs. The next project would take Avro into new territory. It would push the limits of what aircraft could do. Zura was named as the pilot of the Avro Arrow.

Chapter 7
Genesis of the Arrow

It was November 6, 1956. Alarms bells clanged at Air Defence Command (ADC) radar station at Syracuse, New York. ADC had sensed an intruder. The Air National Guard kept two Lockheed F-94BStarfire fighters on alert. Lieutenant Colonel Curtis J. Irwin was commanding officer. As the alarm sounded, Irwin ran out to one of the fighters. Second Lieutenant Gordon W. Simonds was strapping up in the second fighter. They had to intercept a fast-moving target over Lake Ontario. Its speed was more than Mach 1.

Irwin's radar operator called out. "It's gone, Sir! The blip just disappeared off the screen."

It was true. The target had vanished. ADC didn't realize that the target had been a free-flight test model of the Avro Arrow. There was a whole series of these models. A Nike rocket booster launched each model from the test site at Point Petrie, Ontario. This one had been named FFM-8. It had crashed and broken apart in Lake Ontario. The model was made of magnesium alloy. It was painted white with a red rudder and a black number "8." During its 40-second flight, it reached Mach 1.7. Each model was one-eighth-scale and carried two FM transmitters. They provided **telemetry** to a ground station. FFM-8 had sent a burst of data. These data gave readings on the model before it crashed.

The Avro Arrow was to be a supersonic fighter. Tests had to be done with scale models before it could be produced. Most models were used for wind tunnel and water tests. Flight tests checked drag and stability. Eleven free-flight tests would show that the design of the CF-105 was the right one.

The Avro CF-105 Arrow was an interceptor. An interceptor is a fighter plane designed to search and destroy enemy aircraft. It was made of steel, titanium, and aluminum. It was sleek and powerful. The CF-105 was designed to fly faster and higher than anything in the skies. It combined all of the latest technology into a streamlined dart. To see it fly was breathtaking. Even today, few aircraft are its equal.

Plans for the CF-105 began back in 1948. The RCAF

wanted a follow-up for the CF-100, so Avro Canada designed the CF-103. It used the latest swept-wing technology. A sharply angled wing was better at high speeds. A CF-100 fuselage was combined with the swept-wing and tail surfaces. It went to mock-up stage by 1951. However, this design performed only slightly better, and the CF-103 was abandoned.

The RCAF looked at fighters in the United Kingdom, France, and the United States. They even looked at projects that were still in the design stage. The RCAF needed an advanced supersonic interceptor. Did a design exist that could meet their needs?

The RCAF set out its requirements in April 1953. The RCAF interceptor would be able to:
• Fly in Canada's Arctic
• Have two engines for safety
• Carry an advanced weapon system
• Be crewed by a pilot and a navigator
• Operate from a 6000-foot runway
• Be capable of increasing speed to Mach 1.5
• Manoeuvre at 50,000 feet without loss of speed or altitude
• Have a range of 600 nautical miles

Avro's design office studied these requirements. They laid out a series of new designs. Floyd and Chamberlin looked at rocket and turbojet engines. They thought about swept-wing and delta wings. Then they submitted a final proposal for the C-105. Two Rolls-Royce RB-106 or two Curtiss-Wright turbojet YJ67W engines would power it. They would be fitted with afterburners. The C-105 would have delta wings and sleek contours. Missiles would be housed inside the aircraft. It would use an advanced avionics and weapons targeting system.

The military liked the design proposal. In December 1953, the Canadian government put up the money for two C-105 prototype aircraft. The C-105 was soon renamed the CF-105, also called "The Arrow."

The design team had to think about weight and performance. It needed to be a large aircraft and be able to carry enough fuel and weapons. It had to be able to fly high and fast enough for the RCAF. The design team chose a thin delta wing. The weapons were hidden to streamline the shape of the plane. There wasn't enough room to stow the undercarriage so a new design retracted the landing gear into the wing. The design also included plans for maintenance and servicing. The weapons bay could be easily removed on the ground. The engines could be pulled out of the rear fuselage in minutes.

This would be the first aircraft to use titanium in important areas of the structure. Flying at Mach 2 generated a lot of heat. New materials were needed to withstand it. The CF-105 would be first to use electronic controls. The test aircraft would also be loaded with electronic signalling devices. They are known today as black boxes. All of these elements would come together in the final design.

During this time, Avro Canada became a busy place. Avro Aircraft Ltd. made more CF-100s. Avro Orenda Engines began to make increasing numbers of Orenda series of engines. Avro had to expand both divisions. More than 15,000 employees worked at Malton. More than 400 sub-contractors helped supply parts.

Avro's parent company, Hawker-Siddeley Group, began to invest a great deal of money in Canada. By 1954, Avro Canada had expanded. It was into shipping, steel products, truck and bus transportation. It was also into iron and coal mining, railway cars, computers, and electronics. Avro Canada controlled more than 44 companies. It had more than 50,000 employees in all. Annual sales from all of its companies were $450 million. Avro Canada was the third-largest operation in Canada. The new company motto was "The Next Big Step."

Sadly, Avro's first great project came to an end. The Jetliner was cancelled. The only test model was used as a camera platform for aerial photographs. There were no prospects for future orders, so the Jetliner was scrapped.

Cancelling the Jetliner was bad timing. Its rival, the Comet, was withdrawn from service. The Boeing 707 had still not entered regular service. Avro had wanted to manufacture airliners, but when the Jetliner program ended, these dreams fizzled.

Avro was banking its future on the CF-105 Arrow

project. There was excitement in every department. This was not just another aircraft project. The Avro Arrow began to take on a life of its own. Employees thought it was an honour to work on the Arrow. When "the Great Zura" was assigned to the Arrow team, he was flattered. And what a team it was!

Avro gathered the "best of the best" in every area. Crawford Gordon and Fred Smye led the management team. James Floyd took charge of the design. Jim Chamberlin led the aerodynamic research. Wilf Farrance oversaw the internal systems design. Harvey R. Smith, head of manufacturing, developed a new system. It was based on the "Cook-Craigie Plan." It eliminated a prototype stage. This shortened production time. Charles Grinyer at Orenda began work on an advanced new engine to power the Arrow. It would be the mighty Iroquois.

Top engineers and technicians were needed in the design of the CF-105 Arrow. William Dickie hired the best in Canada, in the United States, and in the United Kingdom. Scores of British families made their way to Canada during the 1950s. Their reason for coming was the Avro Arrow project.

Employees lived in the village of Malton. They also lived in the surrounding townships around Toronto. They became "company towns." Avro families lived throughout southern Ontario.

It didn't matter where Avro people worked. They

were proud of what they did. The employees of Avro called themselves "Avroites." Their future looked bright indeed.

However, dark clouds were gathering in Saskatchewan. John George Diefenbaker was the head of the Progressive Conservative Party. He had just become the leader of the opposition. Diefenbaker was the champion of the West. He was ready to become the new prime minister of Canada in 1956.

Chapter 8
Flying the Arrow

March 25, 1958, was a Tuesday morning. The Avro Aircraft plant in Malton was busy. Employees were hard at work preparing the Avro Arrow for its first flight. There was lots of talk among staff members. Rumours said the new bird would fly that day.

However, few Avro employees knew for sure. One was "Shorty" Hatton, chief inspector for test flights. The mechanical checks had to be done. The test pilot had to check the plane. Then Shorty would clear the Arrow for flight.

Jan Zurakowski was the chief test pilot. He had the last call as to whether the Avro Arrow was ready to fly. Tuesday morning was cool and hazy — not the best flying weather. If the forecasts held out, Zurakowski would fly.

The ground crew had been going over the aircraft for hours. Their day began at 6 a.m. Every main part and system had been checked. Zura had to do his "white glove" test of the aircraft. Zura would go over the aircraft thoroughly. The crew was sure he would find nothing wrong. Three days earlier, he had found a hydraulic leak. That test flight had been cancelled.

By nine o'clock, Zura had done his walk-around. He settled into the cockpit. Ray Hopper was the line chief. He peered over his shoulder as seat belts were adjusted. All of the oxygen lines were connected. So were the radio plugs. Zura went through the entire takeoff check-list. When he was ready, he signalled to Doc Staly and Johnnie Straboe. They were to ground-start the Pratt and Whitney J-75 engines. Avro was using these turbo-jets while final tests were done on the Orenda Iroquois engines. There was a shriek. The sound of the jet engines tore through the airport.

The president and general manager at Avro Aircraft heard the roar of the Avro Arrow. He announced that employees could leave their tasks and watch the test flight. More than 7000 employees streamed out of the factory. Word soon spread to the Orenda plant next door. Employees there also joined the crowds outside the Avro hangars.

Before the test flight, the pilots had done computer simulator training. The IBM 704 had defeated the best efforts of all the test pilots. Potocki had only lasted seconds at the controls before he crashed. When the Great Zura took his turn, it was even worse. Avro's computer expert had called in IBM. They were convinced the computer was right. The Avro Arrow would be a disaster. Zura scoffed at the notion. Now that the Arrow was ready for take-off, who would be proved right?

Two Avro chase planes were overhead. Spud Potocki flew a CF-100. Hugh Mackechnie manned the cameras in the back seat. F/L Jack Woodman was in a Canadair Sabre. He would record the flight using a movie camera. The camera was mounted on top of his helmet.

At the run-up area, the Avro Arrow throbbed. Suddenly, the brakes were released. The aircraft began to roll. Zurakowski read off the numbers as the Arrow approached takeoff speed. He reached the one-third mark on Runway 32. Zura eased the control stick back. The nose gear left the runway. The Avro Arrow took to the sky for the first time.

Fred Lake was in the company tower. He announced, "Avro 201 off at 9:51 and cleared to company tower."

The Arrow climbed steadily. At first, it climbed at a speed of 200 knots. Zurakowski tested the plane's controls. He liked how they responded. Then he toggled the undercarriage switch. The gear retracted. A red warning light blinked on. The nose gear had not locked in place. The chase planes closed in to check. The retraction was normal. Zura noted the snag. It was a stubborn light switch. He continued the 30-minute

Arrow RL-201 on its first flight, circling the Avro Aircraft factory.

test flight. The chase planes hugged the Arrow. Zura wheeled back over the Avro factory. He made several formation passes.

Grown men and women wiped away tears. They had worked hard for years. Their beloved Arrow was in the air.

Zura touched down in a slight puff of tire smoke when the brakes bit hard. Behind him streamed the bright red and white drag chute. Zura coasted to a stop in the run-up area. Avro employees greeted him and the Arrow. The flight test engineers and flight crew hoisted

Zura on their shoulders. They carried him to the factory. He was their hero.

On that first flight, Zurakowski had noted only two errors. The faulty warning light and a stubborn air conditioner control. The snag sheet was pinned to the wall in the flight test office. It was like a trophy.

The next round of tests began. Zurakowski flew each of the Avro Arrows as they rolled off the assembly line. Other test pilots began to join him. Spud Potocki flew more than any other pilot. Peter Cope and Jack Woodman also flew the Arrow. As 1958 drew to a close, other Avro and RCAF test pilots prepared for their first flights.

The test program was almost flawless. However, the undercarriage was always a concern at Avro. Dowty was proud of the system he designed. It performed a series of actions. These actions retracted and stowed the main gear of the undercarriage. It was a complex, delicate system. Zurakowski spoke to an official at Dowty. Zura wanted a simpler and stronger gear. On the 11th flight, the right landing gear came down. It did not lock in place properly.

Zurakowski landed normally. With no warning, the airplane skidded wildly to the right. Zura thought that his drag chute had fouled. He released it. The Arrow continued off the runway and into the grass. There was a sickening crack. The right gear leg snapped off. The airplane ground to a halt. The cause was a slipping chain on the rotating gear. Repairs were carried out at Dowty. A stronger, simpler Mk 2 undercarriage was fitted. Zura had been right again.

Potocki also cut off an undercarriage leg in landing. This time, the landing gear wasn't to blame. The Arrow was the first aircraft to use a fly-by-wire system. Electric pulses were used to connect the pilot inputs to control surfaces. Potocki was flying RL-202. When he landed, heavy braking blew out all four main tires. The left main gear leg broke in two as the Arrow ran off the runway. The air force labelled the crash a pilot error. Zurakowski protested. Potocki would never cause an accident.

Two teenagers solved the mystery of what happened. They had snuck inside the factory perimeter. When they were found, their camera was taken away. The boys had taken pictures of the Potocki accident. One of the photos showed that the elevators were locked fully down. This produced a heavy load on the wing. The pictures backed up what Zurakowski found in the data for the flight.

The flight control system had briefly reversed itself. It had planted the Arrow down on the ground too hard. Braking had caused the highly stressed tires to blow. When they exploded, they blew off the gear like shrapnel. In time, Zura solved the tire blowout problems. The Arrow's fly-by-wire system nearly killed Zurakowski on a later flight.

It was the first test of the automatic flight control

system. It began with a normal takeoff. Just off the runway, Zurakowski flicked a switch to put the aircraft into automatic mode. In this mode, the aircraft would take over. Instantly, the giant craft began to roll. It headed straight for the concrete below. Zura didn't waver. He flipped the switch off with his thumb and regained control of the aircraft. He was just feet from the ground.

He repeated the test at a safe altitude. The Arrow twisted into a roll again. The automatic controls were shut off. It went back to normal flight. Technicians traced the problem to a faulty circuit. Zurakowski felt that none of these problems was serious. The Avro Arrow went quickly through the first stage of trials.

The RCAF radar tracking station was in Edgar, Ontario. It monitored most of the test flights. This was part of the North American Air Defense Command (NORAD) chain. Zura was on his seventh flight. He dashed from Georgian Bay to Kingston, Ontario. He went right over RCAF Edgar. Engineer Fred Matthews watched flight communications back at operations. He could hear the excitement in the RCAF radar operator's voice. Zurakowski hit Mach 1.52 (1157 miles per hour) on RL-201 during that flight.

The Arrow still didn't have the Iroquois engines. They were lighter and more powerful. Even without them, it was the fastest thing in the sky. Tests showed that the Arrow had achieved Mach 1.98 at over 50,000 feet. There had been 18 months of testing. Flight test operations began plans to set the world's speed and altitude records with RL-206. It would be the first Iroquois-powered version. It was scheduled to fly in late February 1959.

Chapter 9
"Black Friday"

I n 1957, the company was celebrating the rollout of the first Arrow. However, C. D. Howe was beginning to have doubts. Could the program survive? He spoke in the House of Commons. The huge cost of the program had "given him the shudders."

John Diefenbaker was the Progressive Conservative leader. He was also leader of the opposition. He was fiery. He left no doubt about what he thought of Howe and his projects. Diefenbaker was a tough customer. He had shown how tough he was in the House of Commons.

The Trans-Canada Pipeline was an issue that created conflict. There was much debate about the pipeline in the House of Commons. Diefenbaker thought that Howe wasn't considering the cost of some of the projects he supported. Howe had always thought in grand schemes. Still, he knew how much his "prize" projects cost. The Avro Arrow was one of his projects. The opposition argued against Howe. Howe dismissed many of their arguments. This was not a wise idea. Diefenbaker went on the attack. He accused Howe of running roughshod over the House of Commons.

Diefenbaker used the debate in his election platform. He scored a surprising win. He beat the Liberal government in 1957. Diefenbaker was thrilled. C. D. Howe had been defeated in his home riding. The Progressive Conservatives formed the government, and Diefenbaker became prime minister.

The new government gave the first warning signs late in 1957. George R. Pearkes was the new minister of defence. He reviewed the projects in his department. At the time, there was a growing Soviet missile threat. The success of the Soviet space program and the Sputnik had increased that threat. The United States and Great Britain were working on the manned interceptor aircraft. Pearkes was watching what they were doing. He considered what to do with the Avro Arrow. He talked with the chiefs of staff. They gave conflicting messages. Air marshal Hugh L. Campbell was the RCAF's head. He did not want the focus on the Arrow to change. Other chiefs of staff argued against the Arrow. It would drain money away from other armed forces' programs. Pearkes had to make the decision.

The NORAD agreement had been signed early in

Pearkes's term of office. It brought the RCAF and USAF together under one organization. Its focus was continental air defence. The United States had just added guided missiles to its defence bases. It was promoting the Boeing IM-99 Bomarc. It was a point-defence missile. The United States worked hard to promote the Bomarc to Canada. They said it was a better choice than the manned interceptor. However, the Bomarc had problems. There had been failures on test flights. It hadn't been precise in intercepting targets. The United States was trying to save the program. Bomarc bases stretched across the northern border states. The United States wanted Canada to buy into the Bomarc so it could extend those bases.

Early in 1958, Pearkes went to the United States and asked if they would be interested in buying the Avro Arrow. Pearkes came away with a sale, but it wasn't for the Arrow. He had bought the Bomarc. He said it was more cost-effective to buy an "off-the-shelf" weapon. The United States also provided money to help build missile bases. That convinced the Canadian government. They signed on the dotted line.

When something looks too good to be true, it is. The Bomarc packed a nuclear warhead. When the Bomarc hit, a small nuclear explosion was triggered. The Bomarc was not accurate in its testing. Some said that explosion was the only way a Bomarc could bring down an intruder. Did Pearkes know he was buying a nuclear arsenal? Maybe. Diefenbaker did not. He had made a promise in his election campaign. Canada would help to prevent the increase of nuclear weapons.

The government was leaning towards cancelling the Avro Arrow. Avro Canada's president, Crawford Gordon, realized that. He put up a brave front at head office. The pressures were getting to him. Everyone at Avro Canada needed him to be a leader. However, his world was collapsing around him. He had just left his wife and family. He was drinking a lot. Fred Smye took over the day-to-day work at head office. Smye set up a meeting with the prime minister.

Gordon was furious. Diefenbaker was threatening to destroy the Arrow and his company. As he drank, his rage grew. He stormed into Diefenbaker's office. He demanded that the Arrow continue. He slammed his fist on the prime minister's desk. He screamed out his demands. John Diefenbaker would not back down in the face of a bully. To top it off, Dief was a **teetotaller**. He detested drinkers. Diefenbaker showed Gordon the door. That meeting put an end to any hope for the Arrow. Dief dismissed the whole affair. "I have just told him that the thing is off."

Three days later, on September 23, 1958, John Diefenbaker made a public statement about the Arrow. The Avro Arrow program was being reviewed. So were the Orenda Iroquois engines. The fire-control system and missile armament were cancelled. However, he did not say that the program was cancelled. Diefenbaker announced the purchase of the Bomarc guided missile. Reporters read their own meaning into the statement. The Arrow's time had come.

The final review was delayed until March 1959. At Avro, Gordon and senior management grasped at straws. They began planning a last-ditch media campaign. They wanted to boost the image of the Avro Arrow. Smye warned Gordon. He said the Toronto press wouldn't like it. He was right. The media crucified the Arrow.

In 1958, the public had different opinions about the Arrow. The people in southern Ontario wanted the Arrow program to carry on. They needed the aerospace and aviation industries for their work and well-being. There was little support for the Arrow in the rest of the country. It cost too much and people thought it was too risky.

Gordon's media blitz for the Arrow failed. It increased the conflict with the government. Diefenbaker saw the media campaign as an open challenge. He raged to reporters that he would not be bullied. The prime minister may have wavered about when to cancel the Arrow, but he didn't waver in his resolve to put an end to the Avro Arrow. Quietly, orders went out to RCAF officials. They were to wind up the Arrow project office.

By this time, Janusz Zurakowski was 44, which was old for a test pilot. He had made a promise to his wife. He would retire at 40. He had stayed longer because of the Avro Arrow. Most of the test program was finished. The other test pilots had checked out on the Arrow. Zura decided to retire from test flying. He would become an engineer in the flight test office. He would still be involved with acceptance trials of the Avro Arrow. Zurakowski was convinced. Testing would prove that the Arrow was the finest interceptor aircraft in the world. His last assignment was to organize a test flight on February 19. Spud Potocki flew RL-203 with a flight observer aboard. It was the only time an Arrow carried a passenger. It would also be the last flight of an Avro Arrow.

Jan Zurakowski was at his desk on February 20. The call came in at 9:15 a.m. It was a *Toronto Telegram* reporter. "Have you heard? Dief's done it. He's cancelled the Arrow." Zurakowski couldn't believe it. He went to the administration building. He cornered one of the executives. He saw the shock on the man's face. No one knew anything. John Plant was the president at Avro Aircraft. He said the decision wasn't coming down that day. The government had promised to make the report final in March. The teletype machine in the main office began to clatter.

Ron A. Williams was Gordon's assistant. He peeled off the printout. It was true. The official notice had arrived. The Avro Arrow was cancelled. Avro executives went to the boardroom. They had to decide their next course of action. Plant felt that everyone had to be let go. He checked with the legal department. There was no other option. At 11:15 a.m., Plant's voice rang out over the factory's public address system.

Everyone there that day remembered the solemn tones of the "Black Friday" message. They couldn't recall the exact words, but Plant stated that the Arrow was being cancelled and all employees were to quit work. They must leave the factory. It was all over.

Stan Haswell was high above the Avro plant. He was completing a test of the CF-100 fighter. He checked in with the company tower for instructions. He was told to come in. There was no need to continue the test. Mike Cooper-Slipper got a similar message. He was also in the air, testing the Orenda Iroquois engine mounted on the B-47 test bed. It was the last time the Iroquois would be fired up.

Employees began to leave the buildings. They stepped out into a blizzard. Bill Beatty of CBC Radio was at the parking lot gates. He said it was like "a funeral procession of hundreds of cars. They were lined up bumper-to-bumper, carrying toolmakers, engineers, and office workers from the plant for the last time."

By the weekend, the huge facilities at the aircraft and engine divisions were empty. The five finished Arrows sat outside the flight test hangar. Inside the factory, a fleet of fighters was partly assembled. They were left in Assembly Bay 3.

The list of layoffs was huge. A skeleton crew of

maintenance and security staff was recalled. For the next weeks, they roamed the plants. How long would they hold even these jobs? In April 1959, another crew moved into the Avro plant.

Armed forces personnel swept through the offices of the Avro Company. They collected all records of the CF-105 Arrow. They gathered blueprints, photographs, models, and films. They had orders from the government. They were to destroy all sensitive material connected to the project.

Lou Wise was head of the photographic department. He was ordered to destroy all of the Arrow material. He did what he was ordered to do. However, he prepared copies of everything. Then he destroyed only the copies in public. On the day after the destruct order, Wise called in some military people. They watched him burn photographic stock, film, and files. The original material was safe. He had made sure of that. He hid a 16 mm film, *Supersonic Sentinel,* in his home.

The same thing was happening everywhere. Some workers stuffed blueprints into lunch boxes. Then they walked out of the factory, right past the security staff. Other Avro employees were clever enough to save small caches of tools and parts. One government official rescued countless pieces of the Avro Arrow and Iroquois engines.

Mac Kuhring was head of the National Research Council engine laboratory. He asked for a complete list of materials. This list would record the development of technology in the Avro and Orenda programs. Pallets of equipment, tooling, assemblies, and manuals were accepted en masse. They were all marked "classified." They were hidden away in the NRC facilities at Ottawa.

John Armstrong was the engineer-in-charge at the Nobel test facility. He carried out the government's orders to mothball the plant. His heart wasn't in it. Many parts of the Avro Iroquois engine survived at Nobel. Ian Ferrar was the chief engineer at Orenda. He made sure that at least two complete engines were kept safe in the Rheem container area behind the plant.

Fred Smye couldn't believe it. The military ordered the destruction of the completed Arrows. The aircraft still on the production line were destroyed as well. At first, he refused to obey the order. The government kept pressuring him. They said there would be consequences for the company if he didn't. Army intervention was threatened in the plant. Smye was forced to permit the demolition.

Lou McPherson was one of a team of Avro technicians. They began removing parts from the group of test aircraft. He used an arc welder to cut the nose cone off RL-201. "It just broke me up to do it. I hated the idea of cutting up this dream we all had. But we had to do it." Another group of workers started taking apart the production line.

Jim Floyd protested. He showed Smye requests from

the USAF and RAF. They wanted the Arrows that were left. The British had a test establishment at Boscombe Down. They sent a proposal. They wanted three completed Arrows along with spares. They would be part of a supersonic project. Floyd had started to plan for a transatlantic flight. He had the planning process just days before the destruction orders came into effect.

Smye had also drummed up support from an assistant secretary of the USAF. The assistant made a promise. The USAF would help keep the Arrow production lines at Avro going. The United States would supply radar, fire-control systems, and missiles. They would also provide unrestricted use of the flight test centre at Muroc, California. These donations would have cut down the development costs of the Avro Arrow a great deal.

Smye got in touch with the office of the defence minister with the news right away. He awaited a reply. He would wait in vain. Later, the deputy minister made a comment on record. As a weapons system, "there never was an Arrow."

The Lax Brothers Scrapyard in Hamilton made a purchase. They bought what was left of the Arrow project from the government. They bid $300,000 for the lot. Their bid included airplanes, jigs and tools, and any related fixtures. The work was done quickly behind closed doors. They were not familiar with aircraft. The salvage crew had brought a wrecking ball. It clanged off a hardened section of a fuselage. Then it bounced straight back and nearly hit the operator. Blowtorches were no better. The magnesium and titanium used in the aircraft would be lethal if ignited. The workers settled on axes and saws. They crudely cut up the airframes. The jigs and tooling inside the plant were cut apart with acetylene torches.

No Avro employee could get close to the salvage operation. Elwy Yost remembered the scene: "I'll never forget one thing, the smell of acetylene torches that were being used ..." He also noticed the few Avroites left in the building. They were crying. It was a heartbreaking end to the dream of the Avro Arrow.

Possible sales of the Orenda Iroquois were also dashed. Dassault Aviation in France had been in talks to buy 300 engines for their Mirage IV bomber. Curtiss-Wright in the United States had entered into an agreement for license manufacture. They were told that all deals were off.

There was one last attempt to save the Iroquois program. Canada needed a new tactical fighter for the NATO "strike fighter" role. It was possible that the Republic F-105 would be chosen. It was equipped with the Orenda Iroquois. Republic Aircraft and Avro presented a joint proposal to the Canadian government. It was submitted in the days after the Arrow was cancelled. They went to Ottawa to make a case. Fred Smye wrote, "... that was the last that was heard of that."

A mystery remains about the midnight theft of the cockpit and nose section of RL-206, the first Avro Arrow Mk.2. Dr. John Young from the Aerospace Medical Centre at RCAF Downsview came up with the plot. He hijacked a flat-bed trailer, which a small crew loaded with Arrow parts. Then they transported the parts across town. The parts were taken to a site where they were sealed off with a concrete block in a corner room. The block was painted to match the surrounding walls. The last remains of the Arrow were kept hidden until late in the 1960s. Then they appeared in the storage compound of RCAF Trenton. Or at least that's how the story goes.

The RL-206 was discovered in RCAF storage. It was taken to the National Museum of Science and Technology in Ottawa. It was placed in the aeronautical collection. Today, all that is left of the Arrow is on display in the Canada Aviation Museum in Rockliffe, Ontario.

Chapter 10
Desperate Times

After the Avro Arrow was cancelled, many people were out of a job. Nearly 15,000 employees had worked at the Avro and Orenda factories. Most would never come back. Many would not find a job in aviation again. Avro was supplied with parts and supplies by 600 sub-contractors. They, too, were hit hard when the Arrow was cancelled. In total, an estimated 30,000 employees lost their jobs.

Sir Roy Dobson flew to Canada. He wanted to take personal control. He met with Diefenbaker. Dobson came away from the meeting with a sinking feeling. The parent company was A.V. Roe Canada. It still controlled vast divisions. These divisions manufactured ships, rail cars, buses, and railway stock. They were also into coal, iron, and steel production. All of these programs needed Canadian government contracts.

Dobson had treated Crawford Gordon like a son. He realized Gordon would have to go. Sir Roy demanded that he resign. He hoped this act would soothe the government. It didn't.

Avro had made submissions for new aircraft projects. Smye hoped they would give the company a reprieve for a time. The public was in an uproar over all of the layoffs at Avro. The Diefenbaker government was upset by this uproar, but the government refused to deal with Avro. Pearkes offered a suggestion to Fred Smye. The company simply had to re-tool. Then it could produce new products. He suggested automobiles. Smye couldn't believe his ears. Converting the factory operation would mean they would never produce aircraft again.

Recruiters from top aerospace companies in the United States and Great Britain flocked to Toronto. They wanted to snag the best staff from Avro. Some even set up shop in Avro's parking lots. They invited many Avroites to hire on with them.

Jim Floyd made a promise to his engineering staff. He would find them other jobs. He was true to his word. Floyd returned home to England. He went to work for Hawker-Siddeley. So did a select group of Avro engineers. They began work on an advanced supersonic transport that led to the Concorde.

Recruiters hired Jim Chamberlin and 25 Avro Arrow engineers for the National Aeronautics and

Space Administration (NASA). NASA was just beginning. Chamberlin became the head of the engineering department. He worked on the Mercury and Gemini projects. Then he developed the lunar orbit mission of Project Apollo. All of the former Avro engineers made important contributions to NASA. R. Bryan Erb helped develop the Apollo heat shield. Owen Maynard became chief of the systems engineering division at Apollo. John Hodge, Frederick Matthews, and Tex Roberts ran mission control. Rodney Rose was in mission planning, as was Peter Armitage. He worked on the recovery systems for Mercury, Gemini, and Apollo missions. They were known as the "Avro group." They had great influence at NASA.

More than employees were affected by the layoffs. Malton and surrounding communities were hit hard. A lot of Avroites felt betrayed. Many simply walked away from their homes. They began new lives elsewhere in Canada. Others left the country for good. Numerous breakups occurred in Avro families. Many suicides were linked to Black Friday.

The day when the Arrow and Iroquois engine projects were cancelled would always be known as Black Friday. It was a dark day. Even so, there were still small maintenance contracts. They were for the CF-100 and Orenda engines still in service. These contracts would mean that 1500 technical staff would be called back.

The research and development at Avro was reviewed

again. None of the work would create new projects. Avro Canada had carried out over 70 percent of all industrial research and development in Canada in the 1950s. All of the projects were cancelled in the wake of Black Friday.

One project in the special projects group was run by John Frost. Since 1954, U.S. military backing had kept "flying saucer" research and development going. A tiny production line was set up in the Experimental Flight Test Hangar. The first prototypes of the Avro VZ-9-AV Avrocar were ready to come off that line. Avro was desperate. As many staff as possible were pumped into this project. The Avrocar team swelled into the hundreds.

Frost's research had focused on an advanced supersonic disk-shaped fighter. It was built in full-scale form in the Shaeffer Building. The Avrocar would be a tiny "proof-of-concept" test vehicle. It would only show hovering and low-speed performance. The USAF and U.S. Army funded the project. Frost looked for army interest in hovering craft. He designed a series of "Avromobiles" and "Avroskimmers." They remained paper projects, never making it past the design stage.

In 1959, the U.S. design office halted the entire program. They said it was because of the chaos at Avro Canada. Frost convinced the Americans to restart the project. He knew that the Avrocar was a huge gamble for Avro. The first ground tests had shown that the test vehicle would barely get off the ground. Dobson would not fund any more development.

Only a few test pilots remained in Don Roger's group. Zurakowski was long gone. Spud Potocki became the senior pilot on the Avrocar. Peter Cope was backup. There was five months of engine testing to be done. Then, the first model was shipped to the NASA Ames wind tunnel in California. The second Avrocar was prepared for its maiden flight.

On December 5, 1959, Spud Potocki put on a specially made asbestos flight suit. He approached the Avrocar with caution. There was no ejection seat. He had practised scrambling out of the pilot's cockpit in case he needed to escape. For the last test hops, three cables had held the vehicle down. Even then, he had struggled with the controls. This was not like any other aircraft he had ever flown.

There were three J69 turbojets housed very close to the two cockpits. Firing them up produced tremendous heat throughout the airframe. Instruments would be baked brown after only a few hours. At least cold weather would help keep the heat down.

Potocki pushed the throttles to full power. He felt the little craft wobble. Then it began to rise. Tiny movements on the side-control stick pushed the Avrocar sideways, then forward. Spud gained some forward momentum. Then he drew the nose up to three feet (1 metre) above the ground. He was still safe. A cushion of air cradled the craft.

Potocki tried a few careful moves. Then he pushed

the Avrocar into a sharper turn. The nose pitched violently down. He pulled back on the controls. The vehicle began to wobble. It pitched forward, backward, and sideways. His control movements could not keep up with the reaction of the aircraft. Potocki throttled back. The Avrocar spun like a tiddly-wink to the ground. It landed on its tiny outrigger wheels with a thud. Frost knew his worst fears were true. The Avrocar was just a hovercraft. That is all it would be. This "hubcapping" effect was created when the pilot tried to fly it out of ground cushion. Most of its handling problems were solved in time. However, the Avrocar was barely able to reach highway speeds at an altitude of three feet.

The Avrocar flying tests failed. U.S. funding ran out. The last of Avro's aviation programs ground to a halt. The supersonic test model was broken up, and the two Avrocars were kept by the U.S. military. They ended up in museums.

In 1960, Dobson and the Hawker-Siddeley Group tried one more time to save Avro. The largest factory in the organization was a "ghost town." This was a problem. They looked at a wide range of new ideas for production. American Motors had proposed that they build Ramblers. That proposal was considered but died in the planning stages. Earl Brownridge was general manager of Orenda Engines. He proposed a new car project. He loved sports cars and thought there was a market for a high-performance two-seater. The design office used aircraft technology to turn out a beautiful roadster with an aluminum body. Brownridge got to sit in the finished prototype. That's as far as the project went.

The design office worked with the Richardson Boat Company to produce a new design of aluminum cruisers. It was based on aircraft materials and manufacturing techniques. A few dozen boats were completed. Then the project was cancelled. The aluminum construction was too complex. It made the Richardson boats too expensive to build. After only a small number of sales, it was clear there was no market for a new luxury cruiser.

The final work in the nearly empty plants at Malton was manufacturing steel pots and pans. It was a humiliating end. This had been Canada's aviation giant. It had been the birthplace of the Avro Jetliner, the CF-100 fighter, and the Avro Arrow. The CF-100 was one of the outstanding all-weather fighter interceptors of the 1950s and 1960s. The sturdy "Clunk" or "Lead Sled" was used for over 30 years in Canada and in the Belgian Air Force. Its service life in the RCAF and Canadian Armed Forces stretched into the 1980s.

Sir Roy Dobson made one of his final trips to Canada. He looked around the A.V. Roe Canada boardroom and did not recognize anyone. On April 30, 1962, the company was renamed Hawker Siddeley Canada. Its operations wound down. Orenda Engines kept making engines in a small part of its original plant. It was absorbed in a buy-out later in the 1980s.

Chapter 11
Legend or Myth?

Men and women walked through the security gates at the Boeing Administration Building. Each one clutched a formal invitation. Most of the older people brought something else with them. Some wore faded nametags. Desmond Todd was a former engineer. He recited his badge number to Laura Cooke. She worked for Boeing Toronto. She smiled and motioned him in. Three hundred former Avro employees were coming back home. This would be the first time in a very long time.

There had been many changes at the Malton facility. De Havilland Canada had taken over the factory site. They had sold the property to McDonnell Douglas in 1967. For 30 years, DC-9 wings and individual parts had been produced there. When Boeing had taken over, there had been little need for two million square feet (186,000 m²) of production space. Only a few areas of the plants were still in use.The massive assembly hangars were still there. Most of the administration area had been shut down. Plans had already been put in place to demolish some of the empty buildings. There were only 400 employees. At the height of DC-9 production contracts, the workforce had been 6000 strong.

Stephen J. Fisher was the president of Boeing Toronto Ltd. On October 4, 2002, he marked an anniversary with a reunion of former Avro employees. It had been 45 years since the rollout of the Avro CF-105 Arrow. The Avroites were in their late seventies or early eighties. They had come from across Canada and the United States. They wanted to stand once more in the spot where the Arrow had been manufactured. This time, there was no Arrow. In its place was a full-scale replica Arrow cockpit and nose section. It was from the Toronto Aerospace Museum. Claude Sherwood had brought it. He had once worked on the real Arrow.

More than 15,000 employees and guests had once cheered the Arrow's birth. On the same site, Avroites returned to mark its passing and to share memories. Always, talk came back to the Arrow and what had happened to it.

Some of the main characters in the Arrow story were present. Jim Floyd, Wilf Farrance, Don Rogers, and Lou Wise were there. Others, such as C. D. Howe, Sir Roy

Dobson, Fred Smye, and Crawford Gordon had passed on. George Pearkes and John Diefenbaker were also deceased. After the Arrow debate, Pearkes had left the Cabinet. National defence issues had slipped from his control. One was arming Canada with nuclear weapons. There had been so much controversy, Dief never completely won the public's confidence back. In his memoirs, he wrote about the Avro Arrow. It began his slow slide from power. In his later years, he never spoke about the Arrow in public.

In recent years, the story of the Avro Arrow has become a myth of its own. There have been many books and movies and even a stage play about the Arrow. A 1997 television mini-series stirred up debate about the Avro Arrow. *The Arrow* introduced many people to its story for the first time. The Western Canada Aviation Museum in Winnipeg was used for the Avro factory. A full-scale model Avro Arrow was constructed for the movie. The finished movie prop looked realistic. It could also taxi on its own power. A number of large-scale flying models were designed for the movie to recreate the test flights of the Avro Arrow.

Avroites didn't like the way real people and events were treated in the movie. Historians thought some parts of it were nonsense. There were different opinions about the film. However, one thing is certain. The film once again sparked debate over why the project was cancelled. People came out on both sides of the argument. The Arrow was too costly and too high-tech. It could not do the mission for which it was designed. Yet the end of the Arrow marked the end of an industry for Canada. It was the end of Canada's military aerospace industry. Canada began to rely on the United States and foreign products. Some mourned the loss of the Avro team in future research and development. Thousands of scientists and engineers left Canada. Most were lost for good.

Those who designed, built, and flew the Avro Arrow all agreed. Their beloved aircraft would have achieved greatness. Janusz Zurakowski made this comment: "It was far ahead of its time. It showed that this country was in the forefront in aircraft technology worldwide. There will never be another Arrow."

Forty-five years later, the debate still continued over the cancellation of the Arrow. Almost everyone was horrified at the decision to destroy it.

A group photograph ended the Boeing Toronto reunion. Outside the assembly bay, there was a full-size painting of the Avro Arrow on the concrete. It was a moving reminder to the audience of the day — the Arrow stood proudly in the sunlight. The passage of time had lessened the raw emotions of Black Friday. But time had not taken away its impact.

Randall Whitcomb is a noted Canadian aviation artist and a former air force pilot. However, he does more than paint the Arrow. He is part of a worldwide network of Avro enthusiasts. They maintain that the Arrow was "murdered" by outside forces. His passion for his subject is well-documented. He defends the cause of the Avro Arrow across Canada. Whitcomb recently gave an address in Alberta. He declared, "Established history and public figures have all claimed that the U.S. had nothing to do with it. I have the smoking gun that proves they did." He stated that he has found documents that show that the United States organized the deed. Perhaps it is true. Not everyone is convinced. However, there is an argument for the U.S. conspiracy. It persists to this day. It is part of the mythology of the Avro Arrow.

One thing cannot be disputed. No Arrows escaped the demolition crew's axes. But one Avro engineer had almost pulled it off.

The date was April 22, 1959. Gerry Barbour was an Avro Aircraft engineer in the lofting department. There, blueprint drawings were scribed on metal sections before being cut out. He was furious at the decision to cancel the Arrow. He was even more enraged by the scrapping of all the aircraft. He watched foreman Al Cox begin the butchering of the five flying examples. As he watched, he planned an elaborate heist. He had access to the high-security area. He would steal a "mule" — a small tow truck. He would tow one of the completed airframes to a horse-breeding farm. He would use the farm as a hiding place. In his plans, he imagined his friend, Lorne Ursel, as the pilot of the aircraft. He settled on RL-204 as his target. This Arrow sat at the end of the row. Unlike RL-205, it lay flat on its belly. The RL-202, RL-203, and RL-201 were in pieces. His early-morning tour of the area confirmed that the RL-204 was intact. Could his plan work? Barbour even talked to his boss, Wilhelm "Woo" Shaw, about it. Was it possible?

He signed in that evening at the security gate. There were no problems. Barbour deked out of the hangar. He slipped into the experimental flight test section. In the dark, he moved carefully along the row of Arrows, He stumbled noisily over the remains of RL-201's wings. Barbour found a set of tools in a tool crib. He prepared a mule. He went back to RL-204 to hitch up the tow bar. He stared into the darkness, trying to make out its shape. Something was wrong. The plane hunched down on its front undercarriage leg. The nose wheel had been cut off. Shaw!

Barbour remembered what he had seen on his morning visit. His boss had taken the foreman off to the side. He left the mule and stormed off in a rage. The guard at the gatehouse greeted him with the request to sign out. He angrily refused and stalked off into the night. It would be the last time he saw the Arrows.

Today, the Avro CF-105 Arrow is only a memory. The nose and front landing gear of RL-206, the outer wing panels of RL-203, and an Avro Iroquois engine are displayed in the Canada Aviation Museum. The chopped-up nose section of the Avro Jetliner sits nearby.

Visitors often marvel at the sleek lines of the Avro Arrow. They are also saddened when they notice the jagged end of the cockpit. Years before, wreckers had sawn and chopped it apart.

At the back of the same museum is a Boeing Bomarc missile. The Bomarc proved to be an expensive dud. It was removed from service after just a short career. It was replaced by the McDonnell CF-101 Voodoo. Prime Minister Diefenbaker had to obtain this U.S. fighter to replace the Arrow. When he cancelled the Arrow, he argued that the Arrow had been "overtaken by events" in the missile age. Cabinet documents have been released recently. They show that Diefenbaker knew that ordering a plane to replace the Avro Arrow would affect his political career. The chiefs of staff demanded a replacement for the CF-100. It was obsolete. The Canadian government had to act. Some military advisors noted that the Voodoo had been rejected earlier. It had been declared unsuitable in the initial development of the Avro Arrow.

As of this writing, the last Avro hangars and Administration Building have been demolished. Janusz Zurakowski had once written, "It is impossible to destroy everything ... Governments and torches can destroy an aircraft but they cannot destroy hope and aspiration, and the majesty of the questing spirit. In the hearts of the people, the dream lives on."

Epilogue

They collectively call themselves "Arrowheads." Some grew up with talk of the Avro Arrow and what it could do. Others have only recently discovered the story of the fabled aircraft. The story of the Arrow goes back to the "Golden Age" in Canada's aviation heritage. All have yearned for its return.

Museums across Canada have begun to devote their attention to the Avro Arrow legend. The Arrow is remembered in aviation collections in Calgary, Hamilton, Ottawa, and Winnipeg. The West Parry Sound District Museum is located at Avro's former Nobel test establishment. It created an exhibit in 2000 called the *Avro Arrow: A Dream Denied.*

Organizations have been founded to preserve the legacy of the Avro Arrow. The most important is the Aerospace Heritage Foundation of Canada (AHFC). It is based in Toronto. Its members include former Avro employees and Avro fans. Recently, one of the Arrowheads' prized Arrow "treasures" has been located.

In 1999, a marine mechanic set out on a quest. Tom Gartshore wanted to recover a test model launched from the Point Petre test range. He used one of the original Richardson cruisers. His side-scan sonar came to life in the choppy waters of Lake Ontario. It beeped out the location of one of the nine metal models. It was buried deep in the silt, 260 to 395 feet (80 to 102 m) below. The recovery effort is underway.

Not far from the original Avro and Orenda factories in Toronto, the Avro Arrow has been reborn. The Toronto Aerospace Museum at Downsview Park has begun a project that will take years. They are working to replicate the Arrow. It will go on display along with the Avro Lancaster bomber. The Avro Arrow replica crew is led by Claude Sherwood. The crew is made up of volunteers. Many are ex-Avro Canada staff. Sherwood found technical drawings that he had "squirreled away" in the final days he was at Avro. These drawings were the beginning of the Avro Arrow project.

The steel-framed replica now has a cockpit and nose section. It also has a fuselage, tail, and various outer wing panels completed. One of the project dilemmas was building the Arrow's complex landing gear. Messier-Dowty built and donated new versions of the original undercarriage units. Associated Tube donated 9850 feet (3000 m) of stainless-steel tube. Sico provided paint. Bombardier Aerospace looked after related tools and hardware necessary for the project.

Sherwood and Paul Cabot, the museum director, had plans for the introduction of the recreated Avro Arrow to the public. They wanted its first test pilot in the cockpit. Sadly, Janusz Zurakowski passed away on February 9, 2004, in his hometown of Barry's Bay, Ontario. He had battled leukemia for years. The

Epilogue

Avro Arrow replica will take its place at the museum in time. Zura will be looking down, perhaps with a sly smile. He will know that the Arrow has finally made it back home.

Glossary

aerobatics: unusual flying movements used to show off an airplane

ailerons: two movable sections on the wings of an airplane that control the plane's rolling and banking movements

airframe: the mechanical structure of an aircraft (not including the engines)

Allies: the countries that fought against Germany, Italy, and Japan in World War II

avionics: electronics used to control aircraft

canopy: the hard plastic cover over the cockpit

convoy: a protective escort

1400 hours: 2 p.m.

hybrid: something that combines the qualities of two other things

lanyard: a short rope or cord

modified: changed

munitions: military supplies such as weapons and equipment

photo-reconnaissance: flights to take pictures

prototype: the first one of a kind

scramble: to take off quickly in response to an alert

spars: the main beams of an airplane wing

Sputnik: a Russian satellite; the first to orbit Earth

teetotaller: someone who is against drinking alcohol

telemetry: a way of sending data by radio

turret: a dome on an airplane that houses a gun

VIPs: very important people

Bibliography

Dixon, Joan and Nicholas Kostyan Dixon. *Made for Canada: The Story of Avro's Arrow*. Calgary: A.V. Roe Canada Heritage Museum, 2001.

Floyd, James C. *The Avro Canada C102 Jetliner*. Erin, Ontario: Boston Mills Press, 1986.

Gainor, Chris. *Arrows to the Moon: Avro's Engineers and the Space Race*. Burlington, Ontario: Apogee Books, 2001.

Organ, Richard, Ron Page, Don Watson and Les Wilkinson. *Arrow*. Erin, Ontario: Boston Mills Press, 1980, 1993 (2nd edition).

Peden, Murray. *Fall of An Arrow*. Toronto: Stoddart, 1978.

Zuk, Bill. *Avrocar: Canada's Flying Saucer: The Story of Avro Canada's Secret Projects*. Erin, Ontario: Boston Mills Press, 2001.

——. *Janusz Zurakowski: Legend in the Skies*. St. Catharines, Ontario: Vanwall Publishing, 2004.

Zuuring, Peter. *The Arrow Scrapbook: Rebuilding a Dream and a Nation.* Ottawa: Arrow Alliance Press, 1999.

From Arrow Alliance Press, Kingston, Ontario:
Arrow Countdown. 2001
Arrow First Flight. 2002.
Arrow Rollout. 2002.
Iroquois Rollout. 2002.

For the true "Arrowheads" out there, don't forget to visit the Canada Aviation Museum in Ottawa to see the Arrow and Jetliner cadavers, the Reynold Alberta Aviation Museum in Wetaskiwin, Alberta, to see the full-size CBC movie *Arrow,* the Toronto Aerospace Museum to see the Arrow replica, the Western Canada Aviation Museum to see the Avrocar movie model, and Zurakowski Park in Barry's Bay, Ontario, to see a life-size statue of Janusz Zurakowski and a ¼ scale Avro Arrow.

About the Author

Bill Zuk is an aviation historian and author whose interest in the Avro Arrow dates back to a time when he was an air cadet. He is an active member of the Canadian Aviation Historical Society and the Western Canada Aviation Museum. Currently, he is the Executive Director of the Manitoba Aviation Council with responsibilities in providing training for the aviation industry in Manitoba.

His writing career began in 1997 when he was involved in *The Arrow* mini-series. He is the author of *Avrocar: Canada's Flying Saucer* and *Janusz Zurakowski: Legend in the Skies.* He also worked on the documentary *Avrocar: Saucer Secrets from the Past,* which was based on his book. He was able to fulfill an improbable dream of actually building a flying saucer, albeit, a movie version. In 2003, he served as the curator of a travelling exhibition, *The Avro Arrow: A Dream is Denied* and directed two film documentaries, *Bearing His Soul* and *Zero Over the Prairies,* for CTV and PBS.

His current project is to bring a statue of Andrew Mynarski home to Canada.

Photo Credits

Cover: Canadian Aviation Museum; DND photo: pages 8, 14, 30, 58.